is it

CHR...
TOO MUCH?

ndy Park, who calls himself "Mr Christmas", has celebrated Christmas every single day since 1994. He drinks champagne, sends himself cards and gifts, and sits down to a turkey dinner after watching a recording of the Queen's speech. Over the years, Mr Park has chewed his way through 150,000 Brussels sprouts, and eaten in excess of 100,000 mince pies, washed down with gallons of sherry.

But all this joyful celebration has not come without cost. Mr Park, an electrician, was advised by doctors to stop his habit when his weight ballooned to over 250lb (19 stone). Mr Park, who is single, confesses he has spent a small fortune on Christmas, adding,

> *"It's hard to find a woman who wants to celebrate Christmas every day with you".*

Might also be something to do with the sprouts, Andy.

Most of us don't take Christmas that far. We may love Christmas, but once a year is quite enough for most of us. In fact, sometimes once a year is *more* than enough! Choosing gifts and wrapping them. Shopping for the food, and pulling the whole thing together on time requires a massive amount of effort. You may be tempted to think, "*Why bother?*"

So if you're in danger of sinking under the strain of Christmas, what follows is a simple formula to help you have a *really* happy Christmas.

RELAX

Headline news: Christmas is not a competition. But it's very easy for us to fall into that mindset.

There's the pain of finding the right presents. We will cheerfully say, *"It's the thought that counts"*—but that requires thoughtfulness from both the giver and receiver! Many parents will feel guilty that they simply can't afford what some children and teens actually want. And it gets harder and harder to find things as we get older. What do you get for the man or woman who has everything?

And maybe we secretly can't help estimating the cost of the gift we get and comparing it with the value of what we've given.

There's the hassle of getting ready. It's not just fitting in all the shopping and wrapping. There are the clothes to wear. The cards to write. The arrangements to make. The tree to buy and decorate. Not to mention the food. Christmas day itself is fraught with anxiety for whoever is cooking. Sometimes it can feel like just another day in the office: you do all the work, and the fat guy in the suit gets all the credit.

There's the struggle to keep traditions. We feel a lot of pressure to "get Christmas right". But many of the traditions we feel compelled to fit in with are relatively recent inventions. Christmas cards, Christmas trees, novelty sweaters and even what's on a Christmas plate are all comparatively new. And while traditions are great to follow—they are not compulsory. Santa's SWAT team isn't going to smash through the window and drag you away for eating goulash instead of goose.

So why do we put ourselves under such pressure? Why do we knock ourselves out for this one day, striving to achieve some perfect Christmas where everyone has just what they want—where everyone is engaged and talkative and happy and there are no upsets. Are we simply setting ourselves up for disappointment?

I wonder if it's because, deep down, we feel the gap between the real and the ideal. We know the life we want. Comfortable living. Good relationships. Enjoyable times. That happy feeling of contentment that things are settled and good. But the reality of everyday life feels like exactly the opposite.

But if there could be *just one day* when everything worked, when no one complained, when everyone was happy, when everyone felt at peace with one another and contented… Then our hope for our lives and our families would be real. Perhaps, deep down, we are saying, *"If I could have just one perfect day—then I could cope with the other 364".*

This frustrated hunger for goodness, peace, rest and love is at the very heart of Christmas—because it is the very reason that Jesus was born into the world at the first Christmas.

Many think he came to impose rules—to give people more to do, a bigger burden to manage in life. In fact, he came to do the very opposite—to offer rest: a real sense of restfulness, not from the muddle and mess of life, but *in* the muddle and mess of life. Jesus said:

> *Come to me, all you who are weary and burdened, and I*
> *will give you rest.* The Gospel of Matthew 11 v 28

Turns out that the way to find real rest and renewal at Christmas is to understand who Jesus is and why he came.

RELATE

Headline news. Christmas is about who we're with, rather than what we give and get.

We've been fooled into thinking that our happiness at Christmas is to do with the *things we have*, rather than the *people we are with*.

The finest roast beast, with all the trimmings, cooked by the greatest chef on the planet is worth very little when it's eaten in silence, or if there is a cold hostility around the table. As one wise man said:

> *Better a meal of vegetables with love than a fattened calf*
> *with hatred.* Proverbs 15 v 17

Sadly, Christmas often highlights something darker. The pain of broken relationships is more real for people at Christmas than at any other time of the year. Even while we enjoy the company of others around the table, we remember those who are not with us, because they have died or are distant from us.

I first woke up to the fact that some people hate Christmas when

I joined a new bank. As the first "telephone and internet only" bank in the UK, First Direct boasted that you could call them 24 hours a day, on 365 days of the year.

"What? Even Christmas day?" I asked the chatty woman on the other end of the phone while I was setting up the account. *"Yes,"* she replied. *"The slots get filled up immediately the sheets are put up in March."* Turns out that people don't sign up for double pay, but because they just can't bear to be at home on Christmas Day.

It is advertised as "the season of joy, togetherness and delight". The TV oozes glitter and good cheer; we expect feasting and fun with family and friends. But if the day does not deliver when so much effort has been poured into it, the result can be deep despair.

But it is quite hard, in the paper-ripping, face-stuffing, bubbly-quaffing whirl, to remember that it's the quality and depth of relationships that really matter. So here's the second step towards having a really happy Christmas—focus on *relating*.

Plan your Christmas around having meaningful time with people. Not around the gifts, the glitter or the grub. They should be there to *serve* and *improve* your relationships with others, not to replace them.

Make the effort to be real with the people you are with. Take time to talk and ask real questions, and to give real answers to your friends, family or partner. Give and receive not just presents, but your time, your attention, your affection—yourself.

If there are children around, hang out with them—get down on the carpet and enter their world. Play with them. Laugh with them. Enjoy the wonder of simple things.

3. REFLECT

Christmas is a good time for improving and developing relationships, but it's also a time for working out where we are—for reflecting on where we have got to. The season marks another year in our jobs, our plans, our life—and especially in our relationships with friends and partners.

Soon after we were married, my wife joined a local law firm, which, it turned out, had a special opening just after Christmas. The waiting room was invariably filled with people wanting to file for divorce. *Why?* Because Christmas throws into sharp contrast what we know our relationships should be like and what they actually are.

And this points us back again to the reason why we have Christmas at all. Christmas isn't just about human relationships. It's also about our relationship with God.

We are all made to love. To love the God who made us, and to love others. But our relationship with God has been broken through our selfishness. We have turned that precious gift of love in on ourselves. This is what the Bible writers mean when they talk about sin.

We tend to focus our attention on the many problems in the world, our country and our lives. But the source of all of them is that we have pushed the living God from his rightful place at the centre of our lives. And Jesus taught that our selfishness and sin doesn't just have consequences now, but also in the world to come. *Did you ever give some thought to what kind of relationship you currently have with God?*

Maybe you think of God as someone distant and barely real.
Christmas tells a different story. Perhaps the most famous verse
in the Bible tells us why Jesus came:

> *For God so loved the world that he gave his one and only*
> *Son...*   The Gospel of John 3 v 16

In Jesus, God has come close—by sending his one and only Son.
Close enough to touch and feel. Close enough to see and hear.
Close enough to make us uncomfortable about the way we have
been ignoring him for much of our lives.

Maybe you think of God as not caring for the world—or for you.
Christmas tells a different story. It is puzzling for us to see a world
with so much pain. It is even more troubling when we have person-
ally experienced grief, disappointment and tragedy. We're tempted to
believe that if there is a God, he does not care.

Christmas is a celebration of God's love for us. He *gave his* one
and only Son to us, because he loves us. And this massive dem-
onstration of his love was finally revealed when Jesus died on the
cross. The price of putting our broken world together again was
the death of his Son. That's how much God loves us. That's how
much he cares.

On the day Jesus was born, the sky shone at midnight as the an-
gels sang for joy.

On the day Jesus died, the sky turned black at midday as he hung
bleeding on a cross. As he died, Jesus absorbed into himself all the
sin and selfishness and soul-sickness of our world. And as he did
so, he opened up the way for us to be brought back to God again.

To have our sins forgiven. To have a fresh start in this life. To enjoy an eternity of perfection in the next.

Maybe you think that God is "just not for me". Perhaps you think you're "just not the religious type". Or maybe you have been put off Christianity by a bad experience of church or some other Christians. Or perhaps, like many people, you are simply bored with talk of God.

I used to feel the same way. But then I discovered that I had been rejecting the wrong thing. When I first heard that God was not distant but had come close in Jesus, it made me stop and think again. When I first understood that Jesus was not about rules or religion but about a relationship with God, it was a complete game changer. I discovered that the Christmas message was good news, not bad—that my natural reaction to it was not boredom but surprise and delight.

When we think more closely about relationships, we are entering the real meaning and joy of Christmas—because God is calling *everyone* into a new relationship with himself through Jesus.

But to have a *really* happy Christmas, we also need to…

RECEIVE

Headline news: Christmas is all about receiving a wonderful gift from God.

You may have received some terrible presents in your time. Come to that, you may have given some. But I hope you won't be spending Christmas with the man who announced in his Christmas cards:

*This holiday season, in lieu of gifts, I've decided
to give everyone my opinion.*

Did you ever wonder why we give gifts at Christmas? We give
gifts because God gave us the most precious gift possible: the gift
of his Son. Each and every gift under the tree is a reminder of the
greater gift that God has given to you and me.

And each expression of delight, surprise and happiness you hear
on Christmas Day is just a glimpse of the joy and fulfilment that
is promised to us if we experience that renewed relationship with
God that Jesus came to bring.

But how do we receive the gift that God is giving us in Jesus?

Earlier we looked at the most famous verse in the Bible, which
starts:

> *For God so loved the world that he gave his one and only
> Son...*

The verse concludes like this:

> *... that whoever believes in him shall not perish but have
> eternal life.*

It's a gift that we don't deserve. I hate it when people ignore me,
or refuse to receive help from me, or are ungrateful when I do
things for them. And yet we are all guilty of doing all those things
to God. Not just occasionally, but repeatedly throughout our lives.

God has every reason to walk away, and leave us to ourselves.
Christmas without him. Life without him. For ever without

him—an eternity without rest or loving relationships. But he doesn't. He freely offers us life… rescue… forgiveness… eternity.

He went to the most extraordinary lengths to reach out to us when we were far away. He paid the greatest price imaginable to bridge the gap between us—when we were his enemies. It is a gift we do not deserve, and yet he freely offers his Son to us, because he loves us.

So if we are to receive God's gift of new life, we must receive it *humbly*—admitting to God our failure, and being truly grateful for his love.

It's a gift we can't earn. This may sound like a stupid thing to say, but gifts, by their very nature, *are free*! It would be crazy to imagine a child tearing the paper off a box under the Christmas tree to reveal a bike or an Xbox or a puppy, and then turning to their parents and asking, *"How much do I owe you?"* And yet this is just how many people think our relationship with God works.

We think that God will only accept us if we pay him—with our good works, or our church attendance or our morals or our money. But this is simply not true. God will accept us, not because we deserve it, but because *Jesus* earned it—by his perfect life, and his death for us. God will freely forgive us because of him.

If we are to receive God's gift of new life, we must receive it *gratefully*—admitting that we cannot earn our way into friendship with God, and that Jesus has done everything necessary for our forgiveness.

It's a gift we receive by trusting Jesus.

We receive God's wonderful gift by believing in Jesus.

... that whoever believes in him shall not perish but have eternal life.

Not just by believing he exists and that he is real—which he is. Not just by believing that he is the Son of God sent into the world to rescue us—which he is. Not just by believing that he rose from the dead three days after he died, and is alive today—which he is. But by putting our trust in his death on the cross to make us right with God.

God is offering you the gift of new life in his Son. You can have a better Christmas if you relax and relate. But you will only have a truly joyful Christmas if you *receive* that precious gift from Jesus. He offers to be your Lord and rescuer as you enjoy *real* rest in they ups and downs of life, as you relate to him each day of your life.

Many people have found it helpful to talk to God about these things. They can trace the start of their new relationship with God from a time they said a prayer similar to the one on the next page.

You may not understand everything. You may even have doubts about whether God is really there. But if you respond to God's offer of forgiveness through Christ, he promises to hear your prayer and answer it.

Why not say the words of this prayer out loud, or in the quietness of your heart, to the Lord who knows you and loves you and is listening now?

Dear God

Thank you for Christmas time and for all the good things you have given to me.

Thank you for my friends and family and those who care for me.

Thank you for your great love in sending your Son, Jesus, to be born into the world.

I'm sorry that I have turned away from you and pushed you from your rightful place in my life.

Thank you that Jesus came and died so that I can be forgiven. Thank you that he rose again so that I can receive new life.

Help me to trust in Jesus and his death on the cross as the only way by which I can be right with you.

Please forgive me, and help me to grow and learn what it means to be a follower of Jesus.

Amen